HOW TO MAKE
A BLINDFOLDED FREE THROW

To Brion —

HOW TO MAKE A BLINDFOLDED FREE THROW

THE ART AND SCIENCE OF GROWING AN AUDIENCE ONLINE

JJ MEADOR

NEW DEGREE PRESS

HOW TO MAKE A BLINDFOLDED FREE THROW

The Art and Science of Growing an Audience Online

ISBN   978-1-64137-336-4   *Paperback*

        978-1-64137-652-5   *Ebook*

CONTENTS

ACKNOWLEDGEMENTS

Before I get into this book, I want to thank you for opening it to the first page. Writing this book has been the experience of a lifetime, and I'm so grateful to have fulfilled one of my long-standing dreams of being a published author. There are many people I'd like to thank, and I'd love to give a special shout-out to a few.

I would be nothing without the support of my parents and younger brother; you three have taught me how to be *me*. It's a blessing to not only be motivated by my parents, but also by my brother Connor.

Thank you Alexa Cucchiara for bringing Creators Institute to Fordham, and being a constant source of positivity and inspiration – none of us Rams would have had this opportunity if it weren't for you.

Thank you to Professor Eric Koester for giving us Creators a process to follow, connecting us with key individuals to refine our work, and giving all of us the platform that many of us have so desperately searched for.

And an extra, extra thank you to Brian Bies: from meeting on your own time to re-shoot my campaign's video, to helping me conceptualize my cover, to tracking me down on a round of edits I was putting off... you're the man.

To all of my former water polo teammates at Fordham, thank you for keeping me around even after I stopped playing. I don't know if I'll push my body as hard as I did with you boys for the rest of my life. To Jill's Cat's Updates, to Fordham Aquatics, to those at The Rival: thank you for being a family away from home. And to all my friends from home, thank you for the mix of curiosity and doubt when you found out I was writing a book—I thrive on being the underdog and know I'm doing something worthwhile if my friends think I won't finish.

An additional thank you to everyone who: gave me their time for a personal interview, pre-ordered the eBook, paperback, and multiple copies to make publishing possible, helped spread the word about How to Make a Blindfolded Free Throw to gather amazing momentum, and help me publish a book I am proud of. I am sincerely grateful for all of your help.

Ed Meador	Tammy Meador	Connor Meador
Julia Becker	Justin Becker	Carl Meador
Lucinda Meador	Jim Long Sr.	Mary Baker
Shawn Long	Alex Teng	Gren Cruttenden
Chris Cruttenden	The Coleman Family	Michele Glasky
Melinda Garfield	Coby Garfield	Jim Long Jr.
Tracy Long	Alexa Cucchiara	Mudassir Azeemi
Bryce Charles	Grant Keesling	Jonathon Cramer
Vickie Stevens	Jocelyn Lewis	Mackenzie Finklea
J. Michael Hay	Linda Beresford	Ian Watson
Donna MacDonald	Colleen McFarland	Lisa Ludwick
Corrine Mix	Carol Curry	Judd Howard
Kian Falah	Randall Louie	Matthew Farrell
Mindy Perkins	Alexa Meyer	Gina Gusikoski
Shari Simmons	Brian Donnelly	Ethan Vandeventer
John Kang	Spencer Wing	Madeline Niebanck
Michael Garas	Ines Faguas	Kevin Chu
Jimmy Yang	Justin Carpenter	Matt Newton
Paula Pritts	Tristen Calvitto	Mary Ann Bentrott

PREFACE

——

"Here's the deal: true relentlessness comes when the only thing you have left is relentlessness. When it seems all is lost and all hope and evidence for success have long since vanished, relentlessness is the fuel that drives you through."

—GARY JOHN BISHOP, UNFU*K YOURSELF[1]

All my life, my GPA hovered around the 3.0 mark. My essay and test scores were almost always at the top of the class, but my grades suggest I am of average academic capability... or slightly below. I've always consoled myself with the fact that the average GPA of American millionaires is said to be 2.9[2].

---

1   Bishop, G. (2017). *Unfuck yourself*. London: Yellow Kite.

2   Avella, J. and Lebowitz, S. (2019). *Valedictorians rarely become rich and famous — here's why the average millionaire's college GPA is 2.9*. Business Insider.

This isn't to say you aren't more likely to receive a high-paying job with a higher GPA, because you probably are. What it does imply, though, is that few top students will achieve the levels of success most of us dream of—or at least that's what I'm told when I Google search this issue.

But first, there's a bigger question.

What is success?

I'm not quite sure I can answer that, because it really is different for everybody. All I know is this: my version of success, and the version of more than just a handful of my generation, doesn't quite stack up to the past.

So, at 22 years old and having been born in 1997, what is MY version of success?

At the top, of course, is health and happiness for the people I care about. If I got a phone call saying my Mom died, no accomplishment would matter at all, I'd be crying my eyes out.

I think that my version of success is to open the door to as many conversations with people who are more interesting and more experienced than I am.

If there is anybody out there who thinks they are too young to start reaching for their goals, you're wrong. When you're young or strapped for cash, fewer opportunities are open to you—that's completely true. But there's always a way. Don't be afraid to tell others what your goals are, because you may have a stroke of luck and meet the person that will help you achieve them.

The path may not be clear, you may not think you have the time, you may know for certain that you don't have the resources—but you really just need to get out of your head and into your life. And when it really comes down to it, losing IS learning.

I've always been a semi-dork with childlike curiosity. I must have asked one of my economics professors 50 times by the end of the semester, "What variable is used to represent electricity?" After probably the 40th time, he told me that school would be a lot easier if I weren't trying to break things. He wasn't wrong, but we are who we are.

What kind of an economics student spends their free time taking social media marketing courses online, and preparing for Google certification exams in a seemingly unrelated field? I may be the only one to raise my hand in a room of hundreds. I don't blame the education system for my own lack of interest, I don't blame anyone at all—I'm just so thankful to have been able to spend my free time learning what I wanted to, often for free.

If I hadn't dedicated thousands of hours to research, testing, and conversations with people at the top of my field, this book would not have been possible. If I'd listened the countless numbers of times I was told I was too young to try, this book would not have been possible. If I'd given up after my multiple failed attempts at entrepreneurship, this book would not have been possible. If I didn't set out on a mission, and relentlessly strive to succeed in that mission, this book would not have been possible.

Let me close out this personal statement by saying one last time, thank you to everyone who is reading. I am so grateful for this opportunity.

If at any point you have questions or comments, you can reach me on social media @jjmeador and I'll get back to you as quickly as possible! I'm most responsive on LinkedIn and Instagram.

INTRO

——

"The pressure to quit was worst that winter around Christmas Time. Our userbase was growing, but we were still in all this debt eating one meal a day... which was usually a peanut butter sandwich. My brother had done a lot on the fundraising and networking side, but now someone has to build it and that's me. I have no engineering background, took one CS course in college, and had no idea what I was doing... then we scaled from 0 to 10 Million users."

-KIERAN O'REILLY

Kieran was the first person I interviewed for this book. So, at that point, I didn't really know what to ask or what to expect. I didn't even know for certain that I was 'onto something' with my book topic.

Then Kieran told me, "I don't think Rory and I have spent any advertisement dollars in our lives on a project. We talked to a lot of YouTube celebrities."

* *

"I want to be a YouTuber."
"I want to be a blogger."
"I want to be a VLOGGER!"

A generation ago, kids grew up with dreams to become doctors, teachers, and astronauts. Those jobs were the pinnacle of success. Secure, well-paying, well-respected jobs. Maybe the pinnacle was being a doctor-Navy SEAL in space, but that's not very reasonable in one lifetime unless your name is Jonny Kim[3].

---

3   NASA. (2019). *Astronaut Candidate Jonny Kim.*

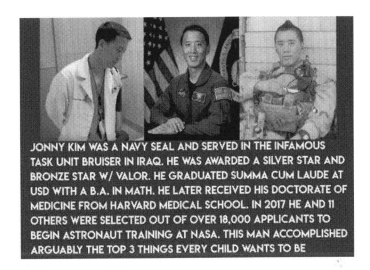

JONNY KIM WAS A NAVY SEAL AND SERVED IN THE INFAMOUS TASK UNIT BRUISER IN IRAQ. HE WAS AWARDED A SILVER STAR AND BRONZE STAR W/ VALOR. HE GRADUATED SUMMA CUM LAUDE AT USD WITH A B.A. IN MATH. HE LATER RECEIVED HIS DOCTORATE OF MEDICINE FROM HARVARD MEDICAL SCHOOL. IN 2017 HE AND 11 OTHERS WERE SELECTED OUT OF OVER 18,000 APPLICANTS TO BEGIN ASTRONAUT TRAINING AT NASA. THIS MAN ACCOMPLISHED ARGUABLY THE TOP 3 THINGS EVERY CHILD WANTS TO BE

But that was never my dream.

In fact, the dreams of the younger end of my generation have changed pretty dramatically.

In this new generation, kids dream of being YouTubers, bloggers, social media personalities, and entrepreneurs. In a recent study, 1,000 kids aged 6-17 were asked what they wanted to be when they grew up. And it found that the top two "Dream Jobs" are[4]:

- 34% want to be a YouTuber
- 18% want to be a Blogger/Vlogger

---

4   Dirnhuber, J. (2019). *Children turn backs on traditional careers in favour of internet fame, study finds.* The Sun.

And if you think it's the money, think again. Creativity, fame, and the opportunity for self-expression occupy the top three attractions of these jobs.... with money in fourth[5].

Today's generation has caught the viral dream.

Just what is the viral dream?

Like many dreams, the benchmark for achievement is subjective and the dictionary definition doesn't lend much help.

"Viral: Becoming very popular by circulating quickly from person to person, especially through the Internet[6]."

The most popular vision I've heard of when it comes to the viral dream is creating one 'thing,' going to bed, and waking up to the world cheering your name. That one 'thing' could range from a YouTube video, to a blog post, to a well-crafted business advertisement.

The core of the story is instantaneous (and fleeting) attention. And we live in an attention-based economy.

---

5   Ibid.

6   www.dictionary.com. (2019). *Definition of viral | Dictionary.com.*

* *

It's impossible to frame my understanding of our digital landscape without drawing from Gary Vaynerchuk. If you don't know who Gary is, this is the perfect opportunity to hop on your favorite social media platform and type in: "@garyvee"

No matter the platform you checked, he's a major player. As an early investor in companies like Twitter and Tumblr, he recognized and executed on what is so special about social media platforms. In his words:

"The cost of starting a business or producing content in today's digital age is dramatically lower than it's ever been. The processor in the iPhone is millions of times more powerful than the computer that first took the US to the moon... If I wanted to produce a long form video show to mirror my vlog, and a radio show to mimic my podcast, and billboards to mimic my images on Instagram, I would have to spend millions of dollars just 20 years ago. Today, the barrier to entry is practically zero. If you have a smartphone and access to the Internet, you are in the game. You can document, create and distribute, at scale, through Facebook, Instagram, Twitter, YouTube, Snapchat, LinkedIn, Twitch, iTunes and many other platforms for pretty much free[7]."

---

7   Vaynerchuk, G. (2017). *Cheering for Optimism and The Internet.* GaryVaynerchuk.com.

The barrier to entry is PRACTICALLY zero. You don't have an audience yet, but you have a platform... multiple platforms. You also have a lot of ways to tackle the next step of growing an audience. So, let's first take a look at Kieran and Rory's path to growing their audience.

* *

Kieran O'Reilly and his older brother Rory have lived my idea of the viral dream.

The brothers were set to graduate high school and spend their next four years at Harvard. Their next four years seemed to be set in stone, until they had an idea.

It started simple: Kieran and Rory wanted to create an app to share short and often snappy videos with friends. Being bright kids, they took development into their own hands... and their friends loved it.

These short, snappy videos are known as GIFs. Whether you pronounce GIF with a J or a G, I'm sure you know what they are. From Twitter to Tinder, gifs from popular movies and TV shows populate all ends of the Internet.

After a year at arguably the most competitive university in the world, Kieran and Rory spent the summer developing their project in arguably the most competitive region in the world—Silicon Valley. They came into the most competitive technology landscape in the world with no connections, no coding experience, no degree, and no money. Just an idea, work ethic, and supportive parents.

Countless late nights, early meetings, housing dilemmas and peanut butter sandwiches later—the time had come for gifs.com to go absolutely viral. By then, Harvard was an afterthought.

Kieran and Rory built a tool that saved content creators hours of tedious edits, and content creators on YouTube are always willing to share their secrets.

"I don't think Rory and I have spent any advertisement dollars in our lives on a project. We talked to a lot of YouTube celebrities about our product, and they loved it. They promoted it. It's like a fire, you just have to ignite it—and that was the spark that ignited the flames," says Kieran.

Soon after, GIFS.com made national news and users were flooding in without any money spent on advertising. The O'Reilly brothers were named Thiel Fellows and part of Forbes 30 under 30, and are now working hard on their next project[8].

---

8   Forbes. (2019). *Rory O'Reilly, 21, Kieran O'Reilly, 20.*

* *

As of writing this book, I have never gone viral.

You might be wondering at this point: Why is a guy that has never gone viral doing writing a book about how to go viral?

I'm going to have to use an analogy that has more to do with sports.

I'm an athlete.

I'm not an NBA-level athlete or basketball player. But I play often and enjoy it.

What is your Free Throw Percentage?

Think of a number.
40%?
60%?
80%?

Why is that your percentage?

I'm going to assume it's based on a couple of factors. The most important will likely be the number of free throws you have taken in your life, the amount of coaching you have gotten to take free throws, and the last time you shot free throws.

Hold on to that number....

Now I want you to imagine a new number. Same thing, you're taking free throws—but this time you're wearing a blindfold.

What's your percentage now?

10%?
20%?
50%?

Why did your assumed percentage drop so much?

Did you suddenly become a worse free throw shooter? Or did you just accept that you won't be as capable of guiding the outcome?

Going viral with an individual post is like shooting a free throw blindfolded.

No matter how much you practice. No matter if you're an NBA player, or a 72-year-old man with a walker, you don't know if the shot is going to go in.

Sure, you can practice all day. You can have the best form in the world. Damn, you can even be Steph Curry—but you can't be sure your blindfolded free throw will go in.

I can't teach you how to go viral with a single post or an entire book.

Nobody can.

What I can teach you, however, is how to shoot a better free throw and how to shoot a lot more of them.

You're blindfolded. You won't even know when it misses, and it will.

A lot of times.

One of the common misconceptions that I would like to address right now is that going viral is absolutely random. This is far from the truth, and to better explain this let's go back to the free throw analogy.

You're taking it blindfolded... but if you've taken thousands of free throws in your life with the goal of scoring, it's more likely that you're going to score one blindfolded when compared to a newcomer.

That's just how practice and statistics work.

As Kieran O'Reilly told me, "The hardest part is taking the first step. If you love what you're doing, you will continue to walk forward. Take the first step and see what it feels like."

* *

This book is designed to help you take steps toward achieving your viral dream. But it's different than many go-viral-quick posts and articles you've seen before. It's not quick and it's not guaranteed.

What I can do is increase the *opportunity* to go viral.

That's the core difference.

If you create a piece of content and it doesn't go viral, you missed. But who's going to see you miss? Just like nobody saw your free throw miss the basket, nobody is going to see the content that didn't go viral.

So, what do you have to lose?

Nothing.

Every failure is a success. And every failure is a success because you have taken another free throw. You've gotten one free throw more accurate. One free throw closer to understanding how to shoot the right way (I like to call these "failures" data).

And one free throw closer to making the shot, and achieving the ever so coveted viral dream.

* *

So once again, you may still be wondering why someone who has never gone viral is writing this book.

I've spent the past four years of my life testing very Instagram growth-hack imaginable. I learned everything about how the platform works. From new updates to Instagram's analytics, to its hourly and daily action limitations, I knew them by heart... and it wasn't enough. I've tested engagement exchange groups, automation, and even apps that promise 'REAL' followers for filling out surveys... but nothing seemed to do the trick.

The closest I've come to going viral are in the form of reposts.

I was shared on Gary Vaynerchuk's Twitter, and the Snapchat story of Tai Lopez—two of the most high-traffic entrepreneurship personalities on the Internet. Neither time did I successfully ride the wave of virality, and within days it was as if I'd never been shared. After interviews with people who have successfully built audiences online, I understand why I've fallen short.

When one post goes viral from a person or brand, it generates interest. When interest is generated, the audience wants to know more about you or your company. They then will browse through the rest of your content on the platform they originally found you on, and decide if your content is worth consuming in the future. Understanding this, we can break content down into its two most important factors.

- Content must have viral potential
- Content must be consistently produced

But beyond all that, you've got to create content to give it the chance to go viral. The truth is that so many businesses and individuals are failing in their content efforts for one major reason:

They are aiming for perfection, when volume is arguably more important.

With numerous platforms to choose from and multiple ways to post on each platform, taking the first step is daunting. Statistics on other companies' success only make the task appear more difficult.

Dollar Shave Club is the perfect example. They spent $4,500 and took a single day to shoot a video that received three million views in mere days and launched the company into the mainstream[9].

Four years later, and the company was sold for $1 billion.

If you're a business owner or content creator looking to follow the lead of Dollar Shave Club and achieve the same results, I wouldn't hold your breath.

You're probably not going to make $1 billion on your launch video. I would, however, urge you to study the methodology of their marketing campaign and those of similar success stories.

Would you bet your life on making a blindfolded free throw?

No way.

But would you bet if you had good form and were able to keep shooting until you made it, that eventually you would?

Yeah, I think so too.

---

9   Blakely, L. (2017). *How a $4,500 YouTube Video Turned Into a $1 Billion Company.* Inc.com.

HOW TO READ
THIS BOOK

———

Hey, my name is JJ Meador... And, by the way, that's pronounced: meh – der.

Before we really dive into this book, I want to introduce myself and give you some insight into how to read this book. Just as importantly, I want to give you some insight into how NOT to read this book.

This book is NOT going to immediately skyrocket your social media accounts to 'influencer' status, or blow up your website with traffic overnight. I can't guarantee that will happen... and I can't guarantee how long this process will take. What

I can do is give you some tips that will make it more likely for you to grow an audience in the long run.

To be transparent: when I came into writing this book, my goal was to learn how people, products, and brands go viral on the Internet with a single post. Writing this book was a huge learning experience for me. One of my early breakthroughs was recognizing that I was trying to answer the wrong question. Working for the long term is more important and more reliable than aiming for a short-lived blip of traffic.

You may feel like this book is a tad disorganized—and let me offer an explanation. I began writing a book on how to go viral, and learned that it should be a book on how to create a system to produce consistent, high-quality content. I also began writing a book where I wanted to explain the intricacies of each social media platform, and learned that it should be a book that focuses on evergreen, easily digestible, platform-agnostic techniques.

If you feel like there are gaps in the fluidity of this book, think of it as my gift to you. As I went through my rounds of edits, I aimed to:

- Brief you on the methods that seem promising, but will only waste your time

- Make as much of this book as evergreen as possible
- Not include platform-specific tips when I could speak platform agnostically, and why I chose to do this
- Only include conversations, topics, and stories that drastically altered my thinking—and stuck around given the first two criteria

That being said – you'll notice chapters like 1, 5, and 8 are meant primarily to add experiential and academic context to my place of understanding.

As far as the blindfolded free throw goes:

Chapters 2-7 are meant to introduce you to what shooting with 'good form' means to me, and how it will vary from person to person, platform to platform, goal to goal, etc. They're meant to overview commonly used platforms, basic story-structure, and a couple of my favorite viral stories (Dollar Shave Club, Joey Bada$$).

Chapters 9-13 are meant to introduce you to different "volume shooting" methodologies that are used by people who have grown large audiences. These strategies range from having other people create your content for free, to creating real-world triggers, to hiring a team, etc. It will close with my intended strategy post-book, and how you can follow along.

There are multiple chapters I put in the archive during my closing weeks of editing, and that's because I think "less is more," especially when it comes to a book that's introducing a topic that may be new to you. It was difficult for me to scratch more advanced and theoretical concepts that I put a lot of time into...

Guess I'm lucky all of these social media platforms exist, and I'll still be able to share the extra stories with you.

Who's ready to learn how to shoot some free throws?

* *

If you want to get connected before beginning the journey that is *How to Make a Blindfolded Free Throw*, find me on any major social platform: @jjmeador

hint If you message me on LinkedIn or Instagram, I will likely get back to you the quickest!

CHAPTER 1

#TBT SOCIAL MEDIA LOG

———

A flashback to my social media log in college: when I started thinking more critically about how social media impacted my daily life. I was a junior at Fordham University, and decided to sign up for a class called "Social Media."

While the coursework was far from what I was hoping to learn in the class, we did complete some valuable assignments. One of these was a social media log, which I've included, unchanged below.

The purpose of this activity was for us to track and think critically about our daily social media usage.

9:30-10:00 AM: The first thing that I did in the morning was habitually check Snapchat and my personal Instagram account. I watched the Snapchat and Instagram stories of my close friends. I sent exactly 11 DMs to promoters and clubs in NYC looking for information on what to do for my 21st Birthday.

10:00-10:30 AM: By this time, I had not yet gotten out of bed or off social media. I checked my personal Facebook briefly, and read an article on Instagram growth. I then went back to Instagram—grabbing 10 travel photos and messaging the photographer that I'd be reposting on the page for a travel agency that I'm in charge of. I messaged from my personal account.

12-12:45 PM: After an hour and a half stretch of not going on social media, I went back to Facebook/Instagram so that I could post content for The Rival Fordham and Behr Travel. **I prefer manual posting to Instagram rather than using a scheduling service.** This was the first time during the day that felt like legitimate work, instead of pleasure.

1:15-1:20ish: Sitting in the cafeteria with my friends, and I habitually and mindlessly checked Snapchat and replied to a couple of messages I had missed in the past few hours. I'm not the biggest fan of Snapchat personally, but have been enjoying opening up the app to check out its updates. I was drawn to Snapchat due to a conversation among my friend group where I had little to no input. It was an escape from conversation.

2:10-2:30: I spent this time replying on my personal Instagram to promoters/clubs that responded. I also sent another five DMs to photographers whose content I wished to repost on Behr Travel, so I could have enough posts ready in my queue for the week. This, once again, felt like it was for work rather than pleasure.

2:55-3:10: Replied once again to snapchats, and watched Snapchat stories (NBA, Vice, etc.)

5-5:05ish: Checked Twitter, remembered that I don't even really enjoy it anymore, promptly left the app and put my phone away.

6:45-7: Replied to every DM I had in my personal Instagram account, took to Venmo to pay a friend for food that night. While I paid no attention to Venmo's feed (its 'social' aspect), I still used the application.

8:00-8:10ish: Created a Yelp account for Behr Travel, scrolled through some Facebook Engagement groups that I am a part of for Instagram/YouTube/Twitter/LinkedIn/Yelp.

9 (less than one minute): I sent a mass snapchat to quite a few of my friends because I FINALLY WON A GAME OF FORTNITE.

10ish-10:25: Realized I had a lot of snapchats to reply to, got stuck in the app with quick responses from friends and did not realize how long I was on my phone non-stop.

11:55-1:30: Spent WAY too much time watching videos on Facebook. Did not even get close to realizing how long I had been watching videos for, and had to consciously convince myself to put my phone on the charger and try to sleep.

My Phone's Battery Usage for the day:
Facebook: 1.75 Hours on screen
Instagram: 1.25 Hours on screen
Snapchat: 40 minutes on screen
Venmo: 2 minutes on screen

I was not surprised to discover I had spent nearly four hours of my day on social media. It is my hope to turn a deep understanding of top platforms into a career, so the majority of this time was not considered 'wasteful' (at least, that's what I tell myself).

-END LOG-

If you're surprised about my web usage, don't be. I was above the average usage, but not by much. According to Statista, the average American user spends 90 minutes between Facebook, Instagram and Snapchat each day[10].

If you've never kept a social media log, I'd suggest giving it a shot. To make it easier, you can do what I did and keep track of your usage in the Notes app of your phone.

I'd love to hear about what you learn through tracking you own usage, so please share! :)

10   Statista. (2019). *Social networks: average daily usage by U.S. users 2021 | Statista.*

CHAPTER 2

THE MEDIUM IS
THE MESSAGE

———

As a 20-year-old undergraduate at the University of Manitoba[11], Marshall McLuhan wrote in his diary that he would NEVER become an academic—but when you predict the Internet 30 years before it's invented, you can't avoid an academic fate. McLuhan went to graduate school at Cambridge, where he took a deep-dive into the 'training of perception.' Similar to Da Vinci's technological ingenuity, McLuhan had strong media ingenuity and accurately conceptualized how society would function within the yet to be invented Internet.

---

11 Gordon, T. (2002). *Who was Marshall McLuhan? – The Estate of Marshall McLuhan.*

Da Vinci was adept at extending the natural world into scientific discoveries, and McLuhan excelled at extending the human experience to technology. Both of their research was ignored for years after their respective academic careers came to a close. Now, we all know who Da Vinci is, and now, McLuhan is hailed as the 'Patron Saint' of *Wired Magazine*[12].

Terms coined by McLuhan in the 1960s include global village, 'hot' and 'cool' media, and the all-important phrase: "the medium is the message," or 'massage' if you enjoy wordplay as much as McLuhan. Oh, and the phrase 'surfing the web' comes from McLuhan too.

We see how accurately McLuhan understood how the worldwide web would develop in his first book, *The Guttenburg Galaxy: The Making of the Typographic Man*. In 1961, when a single computer still occupied an entire room and the Internet was years from conception, McLuhan already knew that:

"The next medium, whatever it is—it may be the extension of consciousness—will include television as its content, not as its environment, and will transform television into an art form. A computer as a research and communication instrument could enhance retrieval, obsolesce mass library organization, retrieve

---

12 Shachtman, N. (2002). *Honoring Wired's Patron Saint.* WIRED.

the individual's encyclopedic function and flip into a private
line to speedily tailored data of a saleable kind."

In simpler terms, McLuhan knew in 1961 that:

- YouTube, Netflix and video streaming services will populate the web
- E-mail, instant messaging, and video chatting will speed communication
- Google, Bing, and other search engines will answer your questions faster than a library
- Even if you still choose books, Amazon will put almost every library out of business
- Data will become a very, very valuable resource

In a time when technology was even more new and scary than it is today, McLuhan argued that technology does not carry moral sentiment. Technology has no moral bent per se, but it profoundly shapes the self-conception of individuals and society. It shapes individuals because all forms of media require interaction.

McLuhan himself admitted that his work should be seen as a 'probe' or toolkit to approach media with. One of his imperfect, yet effective tools was creating two categories of media. Hot and Cool.

McLuhan made hot and cool distinctions between forms of media relative to how they existed at the time. Hot and cool are differentiated based on how much participation is required by the person who consumes the media. Hot Media is rich in sensory data, usually focusing most heavily on one specific sense. Cool Media provides less sensory data, and requires more conscious participation on the end of the user. Hot Media: print, photographs, radio, and movies Cool Media: speech, cartoons, the telephone, and television (though he argued TV was getting hotter)

It is important to note that 'Hot' and 'Cool' media exist on a spectrum, and refer to a piece of content rather than the platform itself. This active/passive split between how we engage with content differs from today, where interactive media sites dominate user attention. Interactive media in the form of our current social media platforms was not something McLuhan explicitly predicted, but he knew they would each fill unique niches. This led to his arguably most famous phrase, "The Medium is the Message."

"Environments are not passive wrappings, but are, rather, active processes which are invisible. The ground rules, pervasive structure, and over-all patterns of environments elude easy perception[13]," he said.

So what does this mean?

In modern terms, sending someone an e-mail is drastically different than sending that exact same message on Facebook. 'The Medium' can be thought of as 'The Platform' and 'the message' as the media, content, and/or text as it stands. Being a fan of wordplay, McLuhan titled his book on the concept, *The Medium is the Massage.*

∗ ∗

When you are creating content meant for the Internet, it is important to understand how each platform is best utilized. While the medium doesn't entirely dictate how your message

---

13 McLuhan, M., Agel, J. and Fiore, Q. (2008). *The medium is the massage.* London: Penguin Books.

will be received by an audience or individual, each platform nudges, or massages, users toward particular predispositions.

Today, practically every popular social media and Internet platform includes multiple types of media—ranging from hot to cold. Facebook, Twitter and even LinkedIn allow for numerous forms of media interaction with text, photo, and video being the most popular.

With social media being new and platforms still rapidly evolving, shifts are often made to include MORE forms of media within each medium. In an ecosystem that could function drastically differently from week to week, or even day to day, nobody can claim to be the absolute master of all digital mediums.

In the words of McLuhan, "Education must shift from instruction, from imposing of stencils, to discovery—to probing and exploration and to the recognition of the language of forms."[14]

In the words of JJ Meador, nobody can teach you how to be creative. Even the experts don't necessarily have the formulas to success. Post media with intent, measure your results, and make changes until you know what works.

---

14 Ibid.

Before spending years testing each platform, it's smart to learn what those who have spent thousands of hours and millions of dollars 'probing' before us have to say.

Let's start with a brief overview of the platforms themselves.

CHAPTER 3

SOME MEDIUMS BRIEFLY EXPLAINED

———

To align with McLuhan, don't use this as a stencil. Don't let me be the one impose limitations on *what* you want to share, *where* you want to share it, or *how* you want to share it. Just remember, there should always be a reason *why* you want to share your message and *why* you selected that medium.

I'm going to keep my explanations of how to best use each medium short for two main reasons. First—social media platforms are ever changing, making it extremely difficult to keep up with trends across them all. So, it's nearly impossible for me to give you detailed guides that will stand the test of time. Second, the best way to post on a platform can literally change from day to day. For example, when Instagram added the story feature, it completely changed the dynamic of posting. Another shift happened again soon after, with the release of IGTV. This isn't exclusive to Instagram, and is just a part of the digital marketing game.

Before you get scared away by the prospect of constant change, remember that it happens to everyone. If you can figure out the secrets of a new feature before the rest of the world, you can catapult to the top.

As a side-note: if you're worried that the platform you are eyeing has changed from when I wrote this book—feel free to reach out to me with questions and I'll get back to you as quickly as I can. @jjmeador

MAJOR PLATFORM BASICS

Facebook:

- Facebook is meant to be a tool to keep in touch, and *connect* with people you know personally. It's meant to feel homey.
- Content on Facebook, including ads, is driven most strongly by evoking emotions. Because of the way Facebook's algorithm functions and the friends you choose to add, you will most often see like-minded

views on Facebook (though I see my fair share of political battles).

- Top-performing content on Facebook ranges from videos, to long text posts, to photo albums—and anything in between. Facebook is often considered to be the generalist platform, as it can do a little bit of everything.
- 2.4 billion users[15]

Instagram:

- Instagram is meant to be much more *visual* of a platform than Facebook. It's essentially a highlight reel of your best moments on camera.
- Evoking emotion is still key to Instagram's content, but I think the content that performs well is often more awe-inspiring. Rather than like-minded views being a key to content growth, being somewhere and doing something desirable is the key. Instagram is the platform where I'd argue the photo/video are the most important aspect, and the caption is next.
- Top-performing content, once again, ranges from pictures to videos. IGTV also gains some people increased amounts of views because it is a relatively new feature. On Instagram, high-definition pictures

15 Stout, D. (2019). *Social Media Statistics: Top Social Networks by Popularity.*

and videos are much more likely to be top performing. The accompanying captions seem to be trending towards longer stories that either educate or entertain.

- 1 billion users[16]

Twitter:

- Twitter is meant to be a tool to *listen* to how a community feels about a current event, and is extremely useful in live reporting.
- Twitter is the platform of choice for many politicians and journalists, because live-action news performs well. Essentially, Twitter is a platform that is best used to hear how diverse groups of people feel about the same event.
- Topping the list of best content are shares of GIFs, short videos, pictures and opinions on controversial events.
- 330 million users[17]

Snapchat:

- Snapchat is one of few social media platforms that is still used primarily for private conversations. It is a more intimate platform than the rest.

---

16 Ibid.
17 Ibid.

- Businesses and people growing their personal brand can use Snapchat to document small pieces of their lives. Like Twitter, the majority of content posted is happening live.
- There are only two ways to post on Snapchat—picture and video content. There isn't a lot of data that users have access to on Snapchat, but videos perform very well. Users are generally more engaged on Snapchat, and generally keep their sound on while using the app.
- 301 million users[18]

LinkedIn:

- LinkedIn is the only major social networking site that is actually dedicated to networking. It is a social job search platform, which is now a haven for B2B marketers.
- If you are posting on LinkedIn, I think you should be knowledgeable about the topic you're posting about. It's a platform based on credibility, for people with credibility. Be wary taking 'too many shots' before you understand this medium better.
- Top-performing content on LinkedIn includes videos, short text posts, long text posts, and original articles.
- Side-note: LinkedIn is the platform I've been focusing the most time on in the past couple of months, and as

---

18   Ibid.

far as I can tell, is the platform I'll focus most heavily on after the release of this book.

- 303 million users[19]

YouTube:

- YouTube is the second largest search engine in the world, and is meant to answer your "how-to" questions in video form. It's evolved into the 'Google' of video, and is a generalist platform so long as you post videos.
- Content on YouTube is broken up into four major parts: the thumbnail image, video title, video, and description. Successful use of YouTube often is a mix of education and entertainment—and it is great for brand awareness.
- 1.9 billion users[20]

The key to it all is the last bullet point of each platform: the user-base. YOU are the key to these platforms succeeding. Without your attention, they're nothing. Attention is fickle.

If you're wondering why I didn't dive into greater detail on how to use each platform, the next chapter is my long-winded, personal approach toward framing that answer.

---

19 Ibid.
20 Ibid.

CHAPTER 4

2 WORMHOLES TO AVOID, DON'T WASTE YOUR TIME

———

I can't pinpoint the day or location, but it must have been my freshman or sophomore year of high school. Seven to eight years ago. Instagram was new, and it felt like every single profile was run by a kid my age. Most users still only followed their friends because brands simply hadn't discovered its utility. To the best of my memory, I was sitting in a computer room between two classrooms when a friend showed me his Instagram.

Somehow, he had almost three times as many followers as I did. It kind of made sense; Allen was a year older and seemed to know everyone. He had endless amounts of energy and the kid could make people laugh. But those weren't the only reasons why he was so far ahead of me.

Allen An was the first person to introduce me to the follow/ unfollow growth strategy, and likely one of the first to use it at all. He explained to me, "You go to a close friend's page, click on their followers, and follow EVERY SINGLE PERSON."

So I decided to give it a shot. Allen was right, it worked. All of a sudden I was nearly two times 'cooler' on Instagram.

I remember staring at my iPhone that night in awe. I was some random, kind of awkward kid at Northwood High School. I only really knew people in my grade who I'd played sports with or had classes with. And now, people throughout the whole district were following me on Instagram! Cute girls I'd never met before, guys I remember competing against in youth sports, and the occasional out-of-touch friends were now a part of my list. Cool!

It would be a lie to say I was instantly hooked, but I never forgot how powerful that spree of follows was. If I were to crudely estimate, I'd say close to 50% of the people I followed gave me a follow back. Instagram was young, and the follow/ unfollow strategy was just taking form.

Throughout the rest of high school, I juggled a strong interest in social media with two varsity sports, a club sport, coaching a community swim team, speech and debate, broadcast journalism, Model United Nations (shout-out Vadim Rubin), and—more often than not—a girlfriend. I had too many interests and not enough time to take a deep dive into social media in high school. Still, I loved using my personal Instagram account.

Upon graduation from Northwood High School in Irvine, California, I was set to go to Fordham University in New York along with my girlfriend at the time. I was recruited to play water polo, and two of my older high school teammates were also a part of the roster. One of those teammates, Matt Farrell, was very close friends with Allen. Allen found himself living in New York during my freshman year, and we were poised to talk Instagram for another year. Allen was showing me what he had done with his feed, and how it could serve as his 'creative resume,' and it struck me…

"I live in two of the most influencer-heavy parts of the world. I play a sport; my girlfriend and I look great together in pictures (excuse the narcissism). If all these other couples are getting free vacations and meals out of Instagram, why aren't we?"

Without an extremely time-consuming collection of extracurriculars, I finally had the time to take my first deep-dive into Instagram—the platform I had loved for so many years.

Sill, playing a Division 1 sport depletes your energy and free time. I couldn't go ALL IN, but I could start playing around some more. The first thing I recognized when trying to grow again, is that the follow/unfollow strategy was significantly less effective. The age of giving out follows like candy had fallen years ago, and I wasn't quite back to square 1—but I wasn't at square 2 anymore either. It was time to do some more research, and testing.

My single hard boundary going into the process was that I would not spend any money. No ads, no purchased followers, no purchased likes. I was, however, fully willing to use sneaky growth methods. I was a kid, and there was nobody to ask for guidance other than Google. So I listened to what I could.

I probably downloaded 15 apps advertised as 'follow exchange' platforms. I would follow an account, and receive a follow. The ratio was closer to receiving 0.75 followers for each follow, but they all varied slightly. After playing around with each of them, I decided on one app to continue with. "Get Followers." Simple.

When I chose this app over the others, I thought it was so clever. The other apps only allowed you to connect one Instagram account, but Get Followers let you connect multiple. I could create a couple of burner accounts, follow up to the 7500 following limit, and get followers on my personal account for it. Perfect, right? Wrong!

A lot of the accounts I was receiving follows from looked real… but I wasn't the only wise guy using burner accounts to grow my own. Within months, I wound up with a hyper-inflated follower number. I wasn't getting enough likes or comments to explain my followers number, which is worse than having fewer followers to begin with.

Luckily for me, "Get Followers" had a portion of their app dedicated to like exchange as well! All I had to do was put more time into liking from my burner accounts, and I was set. I should have expected that these likes would be just as low quality as some of the followers, but I figured I'd be the only one to notice. I knew for a fact that a large number of HUGE influencers and people who were already famous had likes and followers that looked like mine. I also wasn't spending a dime, so it all seemed okay.

Until you hear the dreaded question from a friend… "JJ, did you buy followers?"

Cue the tantrum...

I technically hadn't bought followers, that was a hard line I wasn't willing to cross. The reason I'd respond with frustration was probably because I knew I was cheating the system. I knew a chunk of my followers were ghost accounts, but I hadn't BOUGHT followers. I would deny, deny, deny... but I couldn't explain the exchange apps I was using because I was plain embarrassed by them at that point. I was using other hashtag, follow/unfollow, and DM strategies to grow, which I was transparent about, but the engagement exchange apps were my not-so-little secret.

At the end of my sophomore year of college, my high school girlfriend and I had broken up, and I was pretty badly injured from a tough water polo season. In other words, I spent a lot of time alone with my phone and laptop. During this time, I was circling back to the follow/unfollow method which had worked so well in years past. I recognized that, although it doesn't work as well anymore, it still works. You just have to do a lot more of it to see results.

At this point, I was working full time—so I couldn't do a lot more of it. It was obvious what I had to do if I wanted to grow using the only consistent method I knew of. I had to twist the rules, and automate following and unfollowing.

I soon had a Google Chrome plugin that no longer exists, where I could hover over a post or profile, click 'follow,' and wait a couple of minutes. The plugin automatically followed every account that liked said post. The tool wasn't able to skip following pages that were clear spam or without a profile picture, but it was fine, I'd just unfollow them later. And guess what? It worked, and I was growing again—slowly, but surely.

I would have been growing faster if I had been posting more content, but being on crutches isn't conducive to living a photogenic life. I was out of doing-mode, and deep into learning-mode. It wasn't long before I discovered Telegram engagement groups, and found a way to automate them as well. Telegram engagement groups work similarly to the engagement exchange apps I had used in the past, but accounts were screened prior to entry. Some people found ways to scam the group and exchange likes from fake accounts, but they would be banned from most of the groups on or before their fifth offense.

Now I had roughly 30K followers, my engagement rate looked normal when I posted, and the likes I was receiving were from high-quality accounts—but I still wasn't growing fast enough. Then I found the tool and forum that changed everything... for the worse. Immediately, it was definitely for the better, and I decided to change my strategy entirely.

Fake it til you make it' is a bunch of bullsh*t. Never 'fake it' on social media, because it's EXTREMELY difficult to overcome the credibility hit you WILL take as a result. It doesn't matter if you 'bought followers' or 'exchanged followers,' it's still fake. The only real difference in the way I did it was that it was much less time-effective, free, and I could retain the deceptive statement: 'I've never bought followers or likes.

So I decided to bite the bullet, manually check every follower I had, and delete the ones I presumed to be low quality or fake. If there wasn't a profile picture, if they followed 4,000+ people, or if they generally felt spammy—they were finally wiped off of my profile for good. "Get Followers" was deleted off my phone, and an ineffective strategy was crossed off of my 'test' list.

But before I move onto the next software I tested which temporarily changed everything for me, I want to let you all in on a free tool that will tell you if an Instagrammer's numbers lie.

* *

Igaudit.io is an Instagram Account Audit tool built for the purpose of separating authentic brands and influencers from the ever-growing crowd of accounts boosted by inauthentic activity. But how does it work?

"We fetch up to 200 random followers for the input user. For each follower, our algorithm looks at things like number of posts, followers/following counts, username, and whether the account is private/public, and outputs a score between 0 and 1 (1 being real). We then average those probability scores across all 200 accounts examined to compute the final result. Note that follower reachability is one of the things our algorithm emphasizes—if a follower appears to be inactive or follow a high number of people, they tend to score proportionally lower, because your posts+stories have a much lower chance of actually reaching them. For example, just because you have a 90% score doesn't necessarily mean 10% of your followers are fake; but if someone has below e.g. a 60%, it's a pretty good indication there's been some fraudulent activity on their account."

Igaudit.io boasts that the output % will be within ~8% of the true value. It will test a random 200 followers each time. If you have a public Instagram account and have not yet audited yourself, I HIGHLY encourage you put down this book and go to igaudit.io right now to audit yourself! If you only have your phone on you, that's fine, it works on mobile too.

Anybody who knows anything about authenticity on Instagram will probably check this tool or something similar before talking business with you, so you're only hurting yourself by not knowing your stats. Even if you have no history of faking likes or followers, any public account gets spammed by the fakes who hope you'll follow back. If your percentage is lower than you'd like it to be, I suggest taking a dive into your followers and removing those who don't quite seem real.

For reference, my igaudit.io score through three consecutive trials is as follows:

Unfortunately, I can't properly cite the above section. After going through my final round of book edits, Ig Audit has been taken down (hopefully temporarily) with the following in its place.

Hello,
My name is Andrew Hogue, and I'm an independent researcher from California - I built IG Audit to help bring transparency to Instagram, and now I need your help.

After serving 2.3 million users, and recent press in <u>Wired</u>, <u>BBC</u>, and <u>Paper Mag</u>, Facebook sent a notice to take down IG Audit. To get it back and be notified when it's back online, sign and share the below petition:

<u>Facebook has been taking anti-competitive measures for years</u> against products they deem threatening. By signing and sharing the above link, you can send a message to Facebook that IG Audit is valuable and should continue to serve people worldwide.

If you're interested in helping in other ways, or covering this story as it develops, please message me:

press@authentique.app

* *

I was first let on to Jarvee by an Aaron Ward YouTube video. Aaron makes guides, tutorials and courses to help people grow their businesses and personal brands on the Internet. His YouTube videos explore the complex automation software, Jarvee. Jarvee is a software you have to pay for, and was impressive enough for me to bend my own rule of never paying for Instagram growth. I wasn't buying followers, I wasn't buying fake likes, I was buying a software that would enable me to grow REAL followers and REAL likes more quickly. I couldn't fully explain Jarvee's capabilities to you if I tried, but I got pretty good at using it.

If you're thinking "JJ, you're writing the book... how can you not explain it..." here's an old screenshot of the adjustable options in the 'follow' tab.

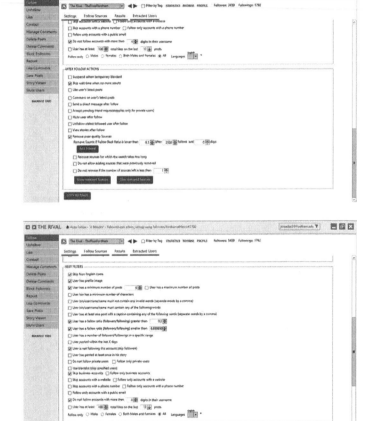

For every other tab on the left (unfollow, like, contact, etc.), the settings are just as intricate. Still want me to explain? Me neither.

It felt good to reach the point with a social media growth tool where Google searches wouldn't teach me anything new. That meant I had learned all that was public knowledge, and either had to start executing on what I'd already learned or find a way to learn more (or so I thought…).

I decided to do both. To execute, I began growing a couple of Instagram accounts in the travel niche. I was growing one for a start-up travel agency, Behr Travel, and four of my own branded travel accounts that I used to test content, new automation strategies, and different follow sources. Jarvee keeps a log of the actions it takes while you are away, and converts them into simple graphs and statistics.

As an economics student with a mind geared towards numbers, this was perfect. I not only had data to quantify my results, but I was also learning new ways to convert social media concepts into simple numbers. I was learning how to teach a computer to act as human as possible, and learning that it takes a lot of corrections. For a while, I thought I had struck gold.

Eventually, I sold one of the four branded travel accounts; one was banned because I posted someone else's content without permission or credit too many times, and two have sat idle for more than a year. I can go back and see stats from a report for one of the accounts I still have access to, and grew inconsistently for a couple of months: @tourism_tbotb. With this account posting inconsistent content and following an automated follow/unfollow strategy, I would receive an 11.9% follow-back rate if I followed the followers of @lifestyleluvquant. But if I used the same strategy on the followers of @unrealholiday, I would only see a 3.2% follow-back rate.

This taught me that it is entirely possible to create an account that is similar to another, and systematically 'steal' their followers' attention. Practically every successful Instagram page fits into a niche, and then further into subniches and locations. I realized that finding source accounts that fit into as many of the same categories as the account I'm trying to grow will yield the best results. I call this "latching."

When I came back to Fordham the next year, my Jarvee abilities were pretty top-notch. It was clear to me that even people filming YouTube tutorials didn't understand the tools as well as I did. My water polo career had just come to an end from my injuries the last season, so I had the free time and passion to find a platform to grow. I wanted to run, or at least help run one of the largest Instagram pages at Fordham.

I was a part of a broadcast journalism and film program in high school, and used to have the goal of becoming a news anchor. Lucky for me, my friend Cole Coyer was a part of Fordham's unaffiliated publication—*The Rival Fordham*. Cole told me I was a little late to apply for the year, but he would expedite the process and send my application directly to the girls in charge. I'm still so thankful they slipped me in past the deadline.

From the first meeting, I felt like I was in my element. I didn't know much about *The Rival* heading in, but I learned:

- As an unaffiliated club, they received no funding from Fordham.

- Because they received no funding from Fordham, they have no topic or content limitations.
- They had a lot of smart and driven students in the club.
- They distribute content primarily on Facebook and Instagram.

When I joined, I had two goals. Get back into making videos, and grow *The Rival*'s Instagram account to reach as many Fordham students as possible. We probably had around 1300-1400 followers when I joined, which is pretty good considering there are only 9,599 undergraduates split between our campus and another. In what I think was an attempt to make me feel comfortable as a new member, I was placed in a 'Rival Live' group with my buddy Cole and three others.

Our group's first video was chosen to be posted for launch, and received the second most views for a video that semester. When I asked some of my friends if they had seen it, they hadn't... nor had they heard of *The Rival* aside from my mentions. Rather than taking that as an ego-hit, I took it as a challenge. By the time I'm done with this, my friends and my friends' friends will know what *The Rival* is and follow the hard work put in by members of the club I now love to be a part of.

As we were gearing up for the second semester, I realized our club's social media manager was a senior. It felt too bold as a member of only a couple months to outright say, 'let me take over next year, I promise we will grow faster than you've ever seen.' So I asked Cole do it for me. I remember being convinced that Cole had some secret sauce when it came to negotiating, because within the day I was put into a group text with the girl who was running *The Rival*'s social media.

I was soon given the passwords to *The Rival*'s Facebook, Twitter, and, most importantly, their Instagram... *our* Instagram. At first, I was just helping the girls in charge, taking over a couple of posts each week when they were busy. *The Rival* had (and still has) roughly two-thirds female followers, so I had to learn how to speak to and speak for a new crowd. I'm still far from perfect at forming content based on the demographic, but a semester of constructive criticism later and I was given the keys to *The Rival*'s Instagram account.

Sitting around 1600 followers going into my senior year, it was time to give *The Rival* some gas. I wasn't creating content anymore, so I wasn't taking blindfolded free throws myself—but the rest of the club sure was. I just wanted to make sure more people would see our members' shots when they scored, and when they missed. All the while, I could watch the statistics provided by Instagram, and understand what shots with good form looked like.

Let's circle back to Jarvee. It's where I "struck gold," after all. If you are trying to grow an initial follower base, it's smart to find 'source accounts' that have a follower demographic as similar to your goals as possible. The audience we desired was Fordham students who follow and engage with Fordham-related Instagram accounts. I didn't have to test different source accounts and settings in an attempt to pinpoint Fordham University Rose Hill undergraduate students; I just had to look for other Fordham Instagram pages.

So I compiled a list of every active Fordham Instagram account, set *The Rival* up with the follow/unfollow settings I developed, and clicked start. Even though my software only executed 20-30 follows in the first day, I knew it had worked immediately. We had close to a 75% follow-back rate on the first day, and the growth would speed up for months before slowing down. Through every Fordham 'source account,' we averaged close to a 35% follow-back rate… making growth three times faster than the travel accounts I was growing.

By the time Jarvee ran out of new people to follow, The Rival was positioned as one of Fordham's largest platforms. Our followers were very real, very targeted, and VERY engaged. The size of our page more than doubled, and now sits close to 3,500 followers. I fully recognize that none of the growth would have been possible if it weren't for the work of the entire club. If editorial hadn't been pushing their writers to create, if the writers weren't on board with providing visually appealing content to post with their articles, and if the producer for *The Rival* Live hadn't pushed the groups to make video content—none of the growth would have been possible. Here's an audit for reference:

I replicated the strategy on a couple more Fordham-related accounts, including a videographer for *The Rival* who started his own Fordham-themed podcast (shout-out Hank Michels and @FordhamFiresides) and a photographer who will be famous one day (shout-out Spencer Krell @SpencerKrell). It worked for them too. The *only* reason it worked though, is because *they* were focused on and succeeding at producing high-quality content.

At the end of this long personal story, let me make one thing very clear.

Jarvee is the LAST tool you should be using to grow your social media accounts at the time of writing.

When I was most using Jarvee's automation tools, Instagram was relatively vague about their rules on the topic. Their long list of rules was directed towards limiting 'spam.' But I figured if some of my accounts were achieving close to a 50% follow-back rate from specific source accounts, that couldn't possibly be called spam. Especially if the new followers stuck around and engaged with content, as they did.

Now, Instagram states their fight against 'automated batch actions' more explicitly, and it's clear that Jarvee is not allowed. It's difficult to leave such an effective tool behind, especially because it increases my favorite variable— efficiency. But there are other ways of being efficient without dancing along Instagram's line of ethical and unethical.

I'm sorry if you got excited at the prospect of using Jarvee to blow up your social media accounts; I was stoked about the tool for a year. I would no longer advise someone to use Jarvee as I haven't used it on an account in quite some time.

＊ ＊

So, what am I trying to teach you with all of this? What did I learn during my years in wormholes learning what NOT to do?

More than one thing. Three, actually.

1. Do NOT go near "The Line"
2. Find and engage your ideal audience
3. Own and re-engage your current audience

My Dad has told me more than once:

"There's always a line. You don't want to go ANYWHERE NEAR that line."

The reason, he'd say, is because the line can move at any time. If it moves, you don't want to catch yourself on the wrong side of it. In terms of social media, that line represents marketing tactics that are and aren't within the platform's rules.

I knew I was getting pretty close to "the line" on Instagram, but I didn't think I was on the wrong side of it… until the rules were changed to be more explicit. This made me realize that the next strategy I devised had to be future-proof.

Don't take this as a limitation from testing new tools that could make your work more efficient; just take it as a precaution.

2. Find and engage your ideal audience

The difference between a 50% follow-back rate, and a 5% follow-back rate is 10X efficiency. I'm not suggesting that you follow/unfollow, but if you find and engage your IDEAL audience – you'll increase your growth ten times over.

3.Own and re-engage your current audience

Your entire goal is to own an audience. Don't forget to continue pushing messages similar to what got them in the door. They are how you will continue your growth.

Much like how professional basketball players all shoot with different forms from the free-throw line, creating content with good form will look different to everyone. But it shouldn't look like either 'trick' I detailed in this chapter.

Instead, your form will differ as you learn how to tell your story.

CHAPTER 5

FRAMED BY
A DIFFERENT
SUBJECT PART 1

———

"At the turn of the 20th century, there was this perception that sharks had never attacked a human being. There as even a reward offered if someone could prove they were bitten by a shark—money that was never collected." [21]

Obviously... that's no longer the case. In 1916, a single great white shark in New Jersey went on a rampage—attacking swimmers on the shore and in a nearby creek. From that

---

21 Choi, C. (2010). *How 'Jaws' Forever Changed Our View of Great White Sharks*. livescience.com.

point onward, public discourse around sharks changed. And as public discourse changes, so does media.

Jaws is often acknowledged as one of the most influential American films ever made, but why is it relevant to crafting your message?

In the words of one of my Fordham professors who works at a major news network, "*Jaws* was so relevant because the 'shark is in the water...' If the shark were killed in the opening scene of the movie, why would you watch it?"

In other words, *relevance* is key to crafting a message that will generate interest. If *Jaws* had come out at the turn of the 20th century, and the public still didn't believe a shark attack was a possibility... I have a hard time believing it would have found the same success. If any at all.

Relevance helps get the audience in the door, but the message itself—the story—is what makes people actually want to share the message with others. There is no single formula for creating the best story, or shooting the best shot. There are, however, five basic elements that can be used as a guide to logically developing your story.

1. **Character(s)**
2. **Setting**

3. **Plot**
4. **Conflict**
5. **Resolution** or **Continuation**

In the same vein as my explanation of the mediums where you can share your story, treat these elements as a guide rather than a restriction. As far as virality goes with a single post, the stories come in all shapes and sizes.

Without further ado, let's take a look at some of my favorite messages that went viral with a single post and see what we can learn.

CHAPTER 6

THE BILLION
DOLLAR VIDEO

If you asked 100 men in America aged 20-30 years old if
they've heard of Dollar Shave Club, I bet the overwhelming
majority don't only know of the company, but know exactly
why they know of the company. Dollar Shave Club, as the
name implies, supplies inexpensive razors and shaving
materials packaged in a subscription box. In other words,
they supply a necessity with a business model that keeps you
coming back.

Dollar Shave Club's CEO, Michael Dubin, is from Venice,
California but spent eight years studying sketch and improv
and was a student at Upright Citizens Brigade training center

in New York[22]. Michael Dubin and Dollar Shave Club were far from the public eye when the company began. As any new business owner that needs to reach customers would do, Dubin devised a video to use as an advertisement. He knew that humor is a powerful device in telling a story, and listened to his gut.

"[Dollar Shave Club] got its first big boost from a 2012 YouTube video, in which Dubin stars, that cost $4,500 and took a single day to shoot. It went supernova-viral in 72 hours[23]."

Michael Dubin was theoretically shooting three pointers and practicing layups his whole life. He then walked to the free throw line, blindfolded, and swished his first shot.

With a background in improv, and business savvy that has shown through continued success—he just needed a product and a platform.

His platform was YouTube, because it was the only place to turn if you were hoping for a video to go viral. Facebook, Instagram, and LinkedIn hadn't evolved into video-dominant platforms yet and YouTube was the most feasible

22 Gallo, C. (2016). *Dollar Shave Club VC: How An Improv Comic Schooled A 115-Year-Old Brand.*

23 Ransom, D. (2015). *How Dollar Shave Club Rode a Viral Video to Sales Success.*

option. Dubin was, like all of us, hoping for his video to go viral. Unlike many of us, though, he was prepared for what came with the wave of virality.

"We also announced our $1 million seed round of funding the day the video launched. We purposely delayed our funding announcement to time it with the video launch and a relaunch of the website. All the usual suspects covered the three events: TechCrunch, etc. From there, the mainstream media picked up on them, and the video took off," Dubin recalls[24].

But it wasn't calculated perfectly enough... and Dollar Shave Club's servers couldn't handle all their new traffic. Within an hour and a half of their video going live, the site crashed. It took them a full 24 hours to get their website functioning again.

"I was terrified that, in that moment, my biggest dreams were turning into my worst nightmares. The next day the site was back up, we had 12,000 new subscribers, and within just a few days, three million people had watched the video."

Michael Dubin knew his audience well, and he knew how to make them (us) laugh. His storytelling ability was amazing,

---

24 Ibid.

and the video included a hook, reputation-building narrative, and extremely relevant value proposition. The release of a round of funding and a rebuilt website coinciding with one of the most profitable viral videos of all time showed preparedness. Even when their website crashed, the team was able to catch the bulk of their virality.

Even if there was money left on the table from the viral video, I doubt Michael Dubin cares at this point since Unilever bought his startup Dollar Shave Club for a reported $1 billion in 2016.

Their advertisement had a clear goal: to build their subscriber list. This is where advertising on new media platforms differs from what we had in the past.

According to author of *DotCom Secrets*, Russell Brunson, there are only three types of traffic on the Internet[25].

- Traffic you own
- Traffic you control
- Traffic you don't control

Traffic you Own

---

25 Brunson, R. (2015). *DotCom Secrets - The Underground Playbook for Growing Your Company Online.* Morgan James.

Your goal with all posts is to own as much relevant traffic as possible. In the case of Dollar Shave Club, they wanted to own their traffic in the form of an email list.

Traffic you control

Traffic you control is that which you pay for through advertising, with the goal of converting it into traffic you own. In the case of Dollar Shave Club, the traffic they controlled was the viewers who watched their promoted YouTube video.

*Traffic you don't control**

Traffic you don't control is everything else. Once your message is out in the ecosystem, you never know who's going to enjoy it enough to share it. You also never know how much the platform's algorithm will push it to new audiences. When you hit the right triggers and reach a large audience you didn't control or own prior to the post, you've gone viral.

Tapping into traffic you don't control is the ultimate goal of someone who's trying to grow their audience without spending a dime. One of my favorite hip-hop artists found a deviously clever way to reach the audience he couldn't afford to control.

CHAPTER 7

THE INTERNET IS SMART, RIGHT?

———

The Internet is smart, right? I mean, maybe not the Internet itself, but the users are smart? Maybe, but neither are THAT smart. Every platform uses its own set of algorithms to determine how to rank its content. These algorithms detect actions taken by the user such as view time, likes, comments, shares, and much more. Something I recognized through my academic background in economics is that algorithms have to make assumptions in order to function. One of the assumptions made by similar algorithms is that users make rational decisions. This doesn't mean that every single individual is assumed to be smart, or even rational. It's just a method to gauge the collective ecosystem.

Here's another one of the reasons I didn't go too in-depth while explaining each platform earlier in this book: social media platforms' algorithms are inherently biased, and constantly changing to account for discovered biases. A way these biases are found is through creators exploiting them. What do you think would happen if a 15-year-old rapper from Brooklyn cracked the code, and tampered with a portion of the ecosystem's rational decision-making ability? Look no further than Joey Bada$$.

Joey always considered Bed-Stuy his home. As a kid, Joey was into Hot Wheels and smashing things before discovering his love for poetry in first grade.

"I remember being in the first grade, and when I was introduced to poetry, I was like, 'Oh, that's the stuff that Biggie does. I love this stuff.' At the time, Biggie was it for me... Biggie was the man, because he was also from Bed-Stuy," Joey Bada$$ says[26].

After cycling through more of the usual childhood desires like video games and sneakers, poetry stuck at the center of Joey's attention. His idolization of Biggie never vanished, but dispersed among other greats like Jay-Z. Now he was in

---

26 Malek, R. (2018). *Joey Bada$$ tells Rami Malek how he uses his music to stand for something bigger - Interview Magazine.* Interview Magazine.

fifth grade, and ready to record original music. He knew the right people to make this happen, but there was a problem.

"My cousins back in Bed-Stuy, they rap too. They were all older than me and I was that kid who was like 'Yo, take me to the studio with y'all! It's not that they wouldn't take me, but my mom wouldn't allow it, because they were into street stuff and she didn't want me to fall into that. That crushed me as a kid. But honestly, that's how I developed the ability to do it myself... Take whatever resources I have and maximize them," he adds.

The negative: he couldn't go rap.

The positive: his mom cared, and was there to help.

After hearing Joey's pleas for video games and audio equipment, his mom gave him an ultimatum. Words I remember hearing from my parents at a young age as well...

"You have to find ways to make money."

After some thought, Joey realized his top skill was cleaning sneakers.

"So I started a little shoe-cleaning business. My mom made 500 business cards—shout-out to Vistaprint.com—and I handed them out all over school."

If Joey couldn't go to the studio with his cousins, he could hustle to make enough money for his OWN studio. Slowly, he saved enough money to buy his first mic, then his second. The next move was to learn how to engineer. Idolizing New York rappers he grew up listening to, his music was reminiscent of throwback 90's hip-hop beats[27]. After hours of practice, and a scheme with some friends—Joey figured 15 was the age he would make it.

"When I was 15, I had this idea of how to go viral. My homie from school had a digital camera and recorded a freestyle video. I got some homies around me amping me up as I rapped. I thought 'because I'm so talented it's going to go viral on WorldStarHipHop.' So I made the video, I edited it myself that same night, and I sent it to WorldStarHipHop probably a hundred times. They didn't put it up[28]."

But it wasn't over. Joey Bada$$, then JayOhVee, knew he had talent that the world needed to see. He hatched a new plan, which you could either call devious or genius. Joey posted the video to his personal account and titled it, "15-year-old freestyles for WorldStar" so when you saw the video you would think it was posted by WorldStar. It worked, and it

27 Breihan, T. (2012). *Mixtape Of The Week: Joey Bada$$ 1999*. Stereogum.

28 Malek, R. (2018). *Joey Bada$$ tells Rami Malek how he uses his music to stand for something bigger - Interview Magazine*. Interview Magazine.

wasn't long before Joey received a DM from his soon-to-be manager.

Joey received the message from Jonny Shipes before leaving for school one day, and gave his mom a big 'I told you so!' A few weeks later Joey brought his parents to meet Jonny, they hit it off, and it was time to get to work. Joey recorded the entire project in his room, and released it with the title "1999."

1999 has received critical acclaim, and launched Joey Bada$$ into the mainstream. It was nominated for Mixtape of the Year by BET, and Joey was hailed as a reincarnation of golden-age hip-hop. He was 17.

"I don't understand Joey Bada$$. I mean, I understand his music just fine. If you've listened to rap for long enough, you understand it, too. It's the sort of warm, dusty, sun-faded boom-bap that New York rap crews were cranking out at a furious rate in, say, 1995. But what I don't understand is how Joey Bada$$ exists. Because Joey was born in 1995. He's exactly the same age as the music he's consciously evoking. What confounds me is that a high school kid from Flatbush is making music this era-specific, and more important, that he's so good at it."

He was 17 years old, and caught the world by storm by merging the old, the new, and the never before seen.

* *

One goal of going viral is to have the RIGHT person see your content, who can change your career forever.

Among many views of Joey's video, Jonny Shipes was the right person.

However, these viral stories don't seem very realistic to the rest of us. I don't know if it's because we can't imagine sending a video to WorldStar 100 times, can't imagine it blowing up on YouTube, or can't imagine throwing a lie in the caption—you're not alone. And knowing how two of my favorite viral stories came about probably doesn't help that much.

But you know what will help?

Learning methodologies to—instead of sending the same video 100 times—test 100 varying videos in a small time frame. Volume, after all, is more important than perfection.

---

29 Breihan, T. (2012). *Mixtape Of The Week: Joey Bada$$ 1999*. Stereogum.

CHAPTER 8

FRAMED BY A DIFFERENT SUBJECT PART 2

"That's how big companies operate. In retail, on television, and on the Internet—companies are looking at lots of products all the time. They all know that, in order for anything to happen, there are going to be lots and lots of trials. The odds of you hitting are very small. Something has to happen that's either very lucky, or very intentional."

—MARTIN SANZARI, DIRECTOR OF ENGINEERING
PHYSICS AT FORDHAM UNIVERSITY

You never know what's going to happen when you put a product or piece of content out there. If you're inventing a product for the first time, it's almost ridiculous to expect it to be a hit. If you're posting content on the Internet for the first time, it's just as ridiculous to expect virality. Much like how a product would go through lots and lots of trials before entering the ecosystem, you should run lots and lots of trials with your audience.

The simplest reason these big retail, television, and Internet companies find success again and again is because: they shoot with good form and they have systems in place to take a lot of shots. And a little luck goes a long way.

Daniel Kahneman, a winner of the Nobel Prize in Economics, formulates success similarly:

Success = Talent + Luck

Great Success = A Little More Talent + A Lot of Luck[30]

Speaking of luck, you're in luck—because the more you develop your talent of effectively telling your story, the greater your chances of getting lucky. In my conversation with Dr. Sanzari, he outlined what good luck looks like in terms of reaching a larger audience, company name omitted:

---

30 Kahneman, D. (2011). *Thinking, fast and slow*. New York: Random House Audio.

"If the right person uses your product, everything changes.

So in this case, it was a women's product. The 'right person' happened to be a writer for a women's magazine. She used the product, loved it, and wrote an article about it. All of a sudden you've tapped into a whole new audience, but you have to be able to follow up on that. They had their website prepared to capture this attention, gained brand recognition, and have successfully launched complimentary products.

I'll give you another example. I came across a product where one of these shows, like Oprah or something picked it up. He thought that his website and everything were good, but they weren't. Now he's hired a team to work on his website and social media, but it's too late—he missed his moment of opportunity."

I know the feeling of getting a blip of traffic, and not being prepared to capture it. It's the worst, but I get it. Rather than having a website optimized to sell and capture leads, the key to capturing new traffic is to have built up an engaging content library.

If posting new content is the best way to get 'lucky' and reach an audience you don't control, and the best way maintain ownership of that audience—it only makes sense to develop a system to consistently post your messages. This section of my book outlines a few different ways to create and implement a working system.

Individual posts give you data, the most valuable resource… but I'd suggest to focus on the long run. There are multiple ways to focus on the long run. But before getting to that, let me go on a mini-tangent about the most valuable resource in the world.

* *

I subscribed to the *Economist* for years, and it was my major source of current events outside of my social media feed for the majority of my life. I still remember seeing the 2017 headline, "The world's most valuable resource is no longer oil, but data," and being mind-blown[31]. Most of the reason I was so awestruck is because I had no idea what this even meant. First off, what did they mean by "data?" And second, how did I not hear about this coming sooner?

I learned from Malcolm Gladwell's Outliers that a large chunk of the wealthiest people of all time was born within just a few sets of time periods[32]. There was often a new industry created, and whoever could take over the new industry would

---

31 The Economist. (2017). *The world's most valuable resource is no longer oil, but data.*

32 Gladwell, M. (2008). *Outliers.* Little, Brown and Company.

be rewarded with immense wealth. One of the periods and industries mentioned was the 20th century oil industry in the United States.

Another period mentioned is the spawn of computers. Data may very well be the next commodity that dominates the economy for a century. Much like the oil landscape, there are some dominant players in the data game:

"Alphabet (Google's parent company), Amazon, Apple, Facebook and Microsoft—look unstoppable. They are the five most valuable firms in the world. Their profits are surging: they collectively racked up $25bn in net profit in the first quarter of 2017. Amazon captures half of all dollars spent online in America. Google and Facebook accounted for almost all the revenue growth in digital advertising in America last year.[33]"

But what does that say about your data? It says that your data is very, very valuable... and you've been giving it up too easily.

For context, let me set a scene.

Imagine you're walking into your local grocery store. You need to get enough food to prepare for a party you're hosting

---

33 The Economist. (2017). *The world's most valuable resource is no longer oil, but data.*

this weekend. You have your groceries in the cart, and head to the line. Before you can pay, or even empty your cart, you're asked to fill out a form with: your name, age, date of birth, e-mail address, home address, and a couple of security questions only you know the answer to.

Doesn't that sound like a bit much?

So why do you give all of that information and more to every website you shop online from?

I think it's a mix of three reasons:

- People don't understand how to protect their personal data.
- It's THAT much more convenient to use Internet services.
- You've never really thought about it, even after the Cambridge Analytica scandal.

I've lived in a world where trading data for free services is customary, and I don't have a problem with it. This is likely because I know nothing else, or because I'm interested in how the business of the Internet operates. Rather than feeling deceived by the high profit made from my data, I want to start collecting data myself.

In an ecosystem that is so strongly dominated by a couple of giants, it seemed impossible for a new platform to thrive. Vine was the closest thing we had to a new platform for years, until it failed. But TikTok is a ray of hope for those looking to compete. It's still possible to create a new platform altogether, though not all that likely. Part of the reason being in the value of data platforms' parent companies have already collected, and its use as a means to retaining our attention.

The data collected stretches past your e-mail address and phone number. When you're with your smartphone, I guarantee that dozens of apps are practically tracking your every move.

"Whether you are going for a run, watching TV or even just sitting in traffic, virtually every activity creates a digital trade—more raw material for the data distilleries. As devices from watches to cars connect to the internet, the volume is increasing: some estimate that a self-driving car will generate 100 gigabytes per second. Meanwhile, artificial-Intelligence (AI) techniques such as machine learning extract more value from data. Algorithms can predict when a customer is ready to buy, a jet-engine needs servicing, or a person is at risk of a disease. Industrial giants such as GE and Siemens now sell themselves as data firms.

The abundance of data changes the nature of competition. Technology giants have always benefited from network effects: the more users Facebook signs up, the more attractive signing up becomes for others. With data there are extra network effects. By collecting more data, a firm has more scope to improve its products, which attracts more users, generating even more data[34]."

That's why people who think about it a lot are worried. When artificial intelligence takes a large leap toward effectively analyzing more intricate data, will it be possible for the rest of us to catch up?

I don't know the right answer to that. I don't think anybody does. But what I do know is that the technology giants conveniently gave users advertisement and analytics platforms to collect and visualize our own data. And if data is more valuable than oil, I know we all want some.

For the sake of growing an audience, let's think of data as your way of determining if your last shot scored or missed. It's a means of improving your shooting form.

---

34 The Economist. (2017). *The world's most valuable resource is no longer oil, but data.*

CHAPTER 9

'GIF' OR 'JIF'?

Kieran O'Reilly was winning. As a senior in high school, Kieran was accepted into Harvard. He wasn't alone, as his (slightly) older brother Rory would be there too. They seemed to have it made—four years at arguably the most prestigious school in the world, and then off to a high-paying job. Their parents were proud, and celebrated by getting two new license plates reading: "2 N HRVD" and "HARVRD 2." Nobody in the family knew that Kieran and Rory's time at Harvard would come to an end soon after it began. Kieran recalls one of his first experiences at Harvard, and told me:

"The first day they have an assembly with one of the Deans, where they say to make your mind an interesting place to live the rest of your life. I think a lot of the students at Harvard come in very ambitious with great ideas, but they get trapped

in the cycle of having to pay back loans and do whatever everyone else is doing... which is counter of what Harvard stands for. The normal college path isn't THAT interesting."

In Kieran's first year at Harvard, his friends ran into a problem. A problem that seemed like it shouldn't exist in the first place. Like many college students, Kieran, Rory, and their friends enjoyed GIFs from popular YouTube videos, TV shows and movies. The problem was, they couldn't text GIFs to each other. In true Harvard fashion, the O'Reilly brothers decided to take development into their own hands.

Their friends loved it.

After spending the rest of the year messing around with the concept and design of their new GIF app, the brothers decided to follow their dreams to the Bay Area. They were only committed through the summer, and had almost no indications of future success.

"When we moved to San Francisco our flight was 13 hours delayed, and we didn't have a place to stay. There are so many interns, tourists and conferences in San Francisco—we couldn't even get a hotel room for a month," Kieran says.

When they flew to San Francisco, they had no connections, close to no coding experience, no degree, no money... they didn't even have a place to stay. They had to figure it out one step at a time. Even after a year at the university many would argue is the most competitive in the world, it wouldn't have been wrong to say that Kieran and Rory were unequipped to compete in arguably the most competitive tech-startup region in the world. All they had was an idea, a strong work ethic, and a brother that covered the other's weaknesses.

Kieran described Rory as a sort of "networking whiz. The taller, smarter, better-looking brother." The second part of that quote may be Kieran's humility shining through, but the first seems to be a hard fact. With great people skills, Rory's primary tasks were networking, securing investors, and developing the overarching vision for their project. Kieran, by contrast, was tasked with building out the project and rolling out updates.

The brothers were making progress, but not without road bumps—many of which were unrelated to the project itself. Without a permanent place to stay, Kieran says, "It was a huge struggle because we'd wake up like 'oh, we gotta move' and things are breaking on our website because we have a lot of users and I'm literally coding in an Uber trying to keep the website running."

Kieran also said multiple times that the hardest part is taking the first step. The O'Reilly brothers were far from the first step—and they knew it. The two realized they were gaining momentum in Silicon Valley, and as the summer came to a close there was only one real option. To drop out of Harvard, and keep on pushing towards their dream.

"I liked school, I had a great time, had lots of friends and really enjoyed my classes. But after our first summer in San Francisco, after creating something, it was like we had a child—and you can't abandon your child."

Their first semester removed from Harvard, the pressure was on. Kieran and Rory had been eating sparingly, sometimes just a meal a day in the form of a peanut butter sandwich. But finally, their user-base was growing. Not only was their user-base growing, but so was investor interest. They were still in debt, but on the cusp of making it big.

Heading into his first Christmas as a Harvard dropout is when Kieran said the pressure was the worst. Rory had done a lot on the networking and fundraising side, and it was approaching Kieran's turn to build out the project.

"I have no engineering background, took one CS course in college, and had literally no idea what I was doing. Then we scaled from 0 to 10 million users," he recalls.

Surprisingly, having 10 million users was still far from where they wanted to be. They were now out of debt, and living in a one-bedroom apartment in Berkeley. Kieran and Rory continued working into what would be their second semester removed from Harvard, when they decided they were reaching a burnout point and needed a day for fun. The O'Reilly brothers' idea of fun was a hack-a-thon at Stanford.

During the hack-a-thon, Rory was approached to apply for what he thought was a $10,000 grant. Rory said yes, for the hell of it, and filled out a form with their information. $10,000 is far from chump change, but being in the Bay Area, Rory didn't pay it much notice. After retaining a steady income through gifs.com for a couple of months, it was time for Kieran to take a much-needed vacation. This time the brothers did not go together, and Rory stayed behind.

"I did a little bit of traveling and when I got back my brother was like, 'a lot has happened since you've been gone.' So Rory was like, 'Biz Stone, co-founder of Twitter, wants to advise us. Our biggest competitor is flying us out to New York, they tell me they want to buy us.' So I'm like okay, that's great. And then he says, 'Oh yeah. We got this e-mail. It says we're finalists, but it doesn't say for what. It says it's from the Thiel Foundation."

First thing's first, Kieran and Rory *had* to fly out to New York and talk to their competitor about a buyout opportunity.

After a friendly meeting, the brothers weren't willing to sell and left ready to keep competing. In the process, they missed the first weekend of info sessions explaining the mysterious e-mail they received from the Thiel Foundation. They still thought it was just a random $10,000 grant.

"We just do this interview thinking it's for $10K, and my brother did super well at it—he talks for like an hour straight. They were like 'wow, we want to have you back!' So, we were invited to the second interview and still confused about what this was all about. At the end they were like, 'let's get dinner.' So we got dinner with the guy who was running it, and they told us they wanted to invest. They wanted to invest, I think like $150K. So we were like, okay, that's great. We have our rounds going anyways. And a few weeks, or maybe a month later, we were finalists for the Thiel Fellowship."

Rory's networking savvy and Kieran's ability to develop their service let them *accidentally* fall into one of the most prestigious college dropout titles in the world. They now had strong momentum, a lot of money, top-notch mentors, and a prestigious title backing their abilities. But, they still hadn't gone viral... or at least not yet.

Whether you pronounce GIF with a J or a G, I'm sure you know what they are. They're short, often snappy videos cropped from popular movies, TV shows and YouTube videos. Gifs populate all ends of the Internet, from Twitter to Tinder, and are considered to be highly engaging content. This may not have been the case if it weren't for Kieran and Rory's website.

Gifs.com grew into a tool that saved content creators hours of tedious edits. It allowed anybody to quickly turn a YouTube video into a GIF. The best part about developing a tool that helps YouTubers turned out to be their willingness to share tools that would make the brothers' lives easier.

"We've never spent any ad dollars in our lives for a project. Instead, we talked to a lot of YouTube celebrities about our product, and they loved it. They promoted it themselves. It's like a fire, you just have to ignite it—and that was the spark that ignited the flames."

Soon after YouTubers began sharing, an article explaining how to use gifs.com was picked up by national news. Kieran didn't feel like gifs.com had officially made it until users kept coming back without remarketing, and new users were still signing up. This mark had now been achieved and exceeded.

Kieran says one the keys to his and Rory's success was to hustle and find their slingshot.

If you're unfamiliar with that phrase, it comes from the story of David and Goliath. Where David, seemingly against all odds, triumphed against Goliath. The 'slingshot' is meant to represent how your perceived disadvantages are actually the key to success.

* *

What was their slingshot when it came to content marketing?

Their product was meant to be used by YouTubers and other content creators. YouTubers and content creators are likely to have audiences of their own. A percentage of those YouTubers who found gifs.com useful shared it with their audience. A percentage of the new audience also consisted of YouTubers and content creators, and the process repeated.

Kieran and Rory didn't spend any money on advertising because they didn't have to. Other people did it for them. As the traffic came, they just had to build their subscriber list.

One method of long-term content creation that can be used effectively is to build a community of people who create the content for you. What a great idea: a product that uses YouTube, helps YouTubers, and is explained in a message that fits the medium.

CHAPTER 10

YOU'RE GETTING BEAT BY AN 8 YEAR-OLD

───

YouTube was estimated to generate over $4.43 billion in 2018, more than 10% of Google's total ad revenue[35]. There is big money involved. With big money involved, you would expect the highest earning YouTube influencer to have a lucrative past. An ex-movie star, big film producer, or some Internet guru would be my first guesses.

In a report from Forbes of the top 10 highest-paid YouTube stars in 2018, numbers 2-10 are populated in descending order by: Logan Paul, PewDiePie, Jacksepticeye, Vanoss Gaming, Markiplier, Jeffree Star, DanTDM, Dude Perfect,

---

35 Statista. (2019). *U.S. YouTube ad advertising revenues 2020 | Statista.*

and Jake Paul. Their content spans from lifestyle vlogging to video games, from makeup art to trick-shot athletics. The lowest earning star on the list made $14.5 million, and just one eclipsed the $22 million mark: a seven-year-old boy named Ryan who reviews toys[36].

The oldest video on Ryan's channel dates back to March 16, 2015 and is titled: Kid playing with toys Lego Duplo Number Train. Not the most poetic title, but I bet you can guess EXACTLY what the video is. The recording resembles a home video, and you can see the outline of a flashlight being used to keep Ryan in the spotlight. The filming and editing are by no means professional. So how did it rack up 47.9 million views to date?

Like any four or five-year-old kid, Ryan loves toys. Like any mother of a four or five-year-old kid, Ryan's mom loves documenting and sharing happy moments spent with her kid. Like any kid of this generation, Ryan loved watching toy review videos on YouTube. Then, like any kid his age, Ryan asked his mom a question.

"One day, he asked me, 'How come I'm not on YouTube when all the other kids are?' So we just decided—yeah, we can do that. Then, we took him to the store to get his very first toy—I

36 Robehmed, N. and Burg, M. (2019). *Highest-Paid YouTube Stars 2018: Markiplier, Jake Paul, PewDiePie And More.* Forbes.com.

think it was a Lego train set—and it all started from there," *Ryan's mom said*[37].

Ryan's toy channel is a part of a larger YouTube trend, but Ryan is at the pinnacle and is the youngest YouTube star we've ever seen. But it wasn't always this way.

Ryan's ToysReview had a difficult time racking up views initially. Ryan's mom was working hard on their project. They were consistently posting content, but for around four months... nothing.

On July 1, 2015 they finally scored their first blindfolded free throw.

The video was titled, "GIANT Lightning McQueen Egg Surprise with 100+ Disney Cars Toys." Once again, nothing poetic or creative about the title... but this time was different. The video sits at 980 million views to date, and Ryan's channel was set to double viewership with each passing month.

Four years of consistent content later and Ryan's last name has yet to be released to the public, with his parents being even more of a mystery. Though Ryan is the star of the show, I tip my hat to his parents for navigating his success the way

37   Schmidt, S. (2017). *6-year-old made $11 million in one year reviewing toys on YouTube*. Washington Post.

they did. In 2017, Ryan's parents signed a deal with pocket.
watch[38], the company that still manages marketing and
merchandise for Ryan's YouTube channel. It paid off almost
immediately, and in 2017 Ryan was the eighth highest paid
YouTube entrepreneur with an $11 million haul in one year.

Remaining largely anonymous, Ryan and his parents not
only achieved the viral dream, they maintained it. They are
constantly making changes in the style and content of Ryan's
review videos. Instead of just a single toy and review, they've
stretched the limits and even created a video with one-second
reviews of 100 toys.

Ryan had a support system that is not at all typical. A mother
who was reportedly willing to quit her job and connect with
a media company to fulfill her kid's dream was likely one
of the keys to Ryan's continued success. Not only did she
support him, but she also took an active role and intelligently
maneuvered the process.

This portrays a larger trend in the industry. There is typically
a single face to a channel, and other behind-the-scenes people
who make it all work. Collaboration is key. Ryan didn't know
how to start a YouTube channel, so he asked his mom. His

---

38 Press, A. (2018). *7-year-old toy reviewer on YouTube becomes a toy
    himself.* Whdh.com.

mom didn't know how to optimize a YouTube channel, so she asked pocket.watch. And boom.

2018 was Ryan's biggest year yet. Pocket.watch developed an app called Tag with Ryan, Ryan began a product line at Walmart, and the stage was set for a 20-episode television series to be produced with Ryan as the centerpiece.

Ryan and his mom took a leap of faith, and stuck the landing. They latched onto a growing YouTube trend, created consistent and purposeful content, and loved their work. It started as simple documentation of mother/son time, and evolved as it gained traction. When there were roadblocks or knowledge gaps, they asked for help. How simple.

So let me ask you... If you aren't succeeding online, is it because a five-year-old and his mom are more capable than you? Do they have more resources than you? More connections? Do they have more luck?

They may be luckier... I can't deny that—but I think it's because they used an interesting strategy to continuously create content. They used a trigger event.

When Ryan got a new toy and was opening it, they would record a video. They didn't have to think about what the next 'story' was going to be; it was just a part of their life.

They didn't have to think about how consistently a new video needed to be posted because they were simply documenting.

This is all very interesting to me, but the story just feels SO sensationalized. SO lucky. That's how a lot of viral stories feel... Like they just got lucky, and we can't do what they've done. But we can.

CHAPTER 11

#HAVEFUN

With a digital landscape full of sensationalized stories and deception, stories like Ryan's don't make ME feel like I can grow an audience of my own. They make ME feel like only the unicorns take off. Really *nothing* made me feel like I could grow an audience of my own, until Bryce Wong.

Bryce was the varsity team captain of my high school's water polo team. As a freshman who was relatively new to the sport, of course I looked up to the varsity team's captain. I wanted to work my way to his spot by the time I was a senior... and I did.

When I realized years later that Bryce's Art had over 100K followers on Instagram (@bbbrycewong), growing my own audience finally felt completely possible. If I could attain his achievement of becoming a team captain, it felt like there was no reason I wouldn't be able to learn from his experience growing an audience and execute it in my own way.

So, as a hopeful creator, I had to ask some questions about how and why he grew his page. And more importantly—why does ALMOST EVERY SINGLE POST on his page include the hashtag: #havefun.

"What I remind myself with #havefun is that: you have to do things that you don't like to do to get paid, get a job, and all that good stuff. Remember to always have fun on the side. I love my job, I love designing shoes, but it's still work. I think when I challenge myself creatively and do my thing on the side, it reflects in my mood and quality of work at the office. I was drawing when we were back in elementary school, you know? It's what I do," Bryce said.

With a resume that includes an industrial design program at the University of Cincinnati, seven internships, a handful of art shows, 2000+ art posts on Instagram, and a footwear design job at Nike—yeah, drawing is what Bryce does.

Rather than creating posts based only on external triggers, like the case of Ryan buying toys, Bryce blocked out time in his schedule for *fun*. It made the most sense to set an earlier alarm than usual, and #havefun first thing in the morning.

Waking up early is a whole lot easier when you're excited about what's getting you out of bed. In high school, that was water polo—for both of us. For Bryce, now it's art. For me, at the time of writing, it's this book.

Bryce was one of the first people I interviewed for this book. As I started the journey, Bryce gave me some advice on something he thinks makes all the difference: "Try and be as kind as you can, have as much fun as you can, and do it because you enjoy it. Everything I do with my art is for fun. The real thing I am is an artist with ADHD, so that's what you'll see on my Instagram."

I'd heard this so many times before, in so many different combinations of words, but it never stuck quite like when I heard it from Bryce. The whole point of working on the side is to do something you're passionate about. Something you don't do for a single goal... you do it because it's fun, and it's who you are.

If you find something fun and it's who you are, you won't struggle to tell your story or to find time to document your journey. Instead, you'll struggle if you DON'T tell your story, or find time to document your journey.

* *

Don't feel obligated to document your journey, but if you're trying to grow an audience online, it's not going to happen unless you do. Art is straightforward to share on social media, especially Instagram, as soon as you finish the piece. But what if YOUR story isn't visually appealing, or conducive to sharing at the time of creation?

Like… a book.

Well, I have a single favorite answer to that question—which I am basing my post-book content strategy on.

CHAPTER 12

ESTABLISH YOUR PILLAR

———

It may seem like a daunting task to post content consistently on Facebook, Twitter, Instagram, YouTube, LinkedIn, Snapchat, etc. But what if I told you there was a strategy to document content for every major platform at the same time? And by every major platform, I'm even including iTunes and SoundCloud.

Would you be interested?

The key, according to Gary Vaynerchuk, is to think in the shape of a funnel[39].

———

39 Vaynerchuk, Gary. 2019. "The Garyvee Content Strategy: How To Grow And Distribute Your Brand'S Social Media Content". *Garyvaynerchuk.Com*.

You begin with a long-form piece of "pillar content." Pillar content comes in different forms depending on your current credibility, niche and personal interests. One of the reasons I'm so excited for this book to get published is because a book is a form of pillar content. Other forms could be a podcast, video of a keynote speech, or just your daily life—as long as it is long-form and contains the message you want to broadcast.

Receiving views on this "pillar content" should be your goal, and different social media channels can be your means to achieve that goal without expensive advertisements. From your long-form piece of content, the next step is to mark the highlights of your video or book, and transform them into media crafted for each respective platform.

In other words, find the best 'micro' pieces of your 'macro' content. You can go through the process of repurposing content for each platform in-house, or outsource. If you are able to produce a lot of pieces of micro content at one time, you won't have to constantly be digging for something to post. You can schedule posts as far in advance as you can stretch your content.

If you'd like a couple examples of how people turn their pillar content into social media posts, I would suggest looking at two people who succeeded with drastically different messages.

If you want a simple way to repurpose written content for the Internet, look at Ray Dalio's Twitter, LinkedIn and Instagram accounts. His book, *Principles: Life and Work* (which I've read and suggest you read as well), is broken down into numbered principles Ray established throughout his life. There are 16 of them, each with their own subsections. Ray posts a new principle each day on his social media platforms, all linking back to his book, website, or app—his pillar content.

If you're looking for more complexity, I'd suggest you look again to Gary Vaynerchuk. The vast majority of his posts are predicated around his Daily Vlog, a Q&A podcast, and different types of interviews. Gary manages to post 30+ pieces of content a day, consistently touching every major digital channel. This is because he is constantly documenting his work life (he literally hired a videographer, DROCK, to follow him around and record him all day), and Gary has a team to craft his content for each platform.

For those of you in a financial situation closer to mine than Ray Dalio and Gary Vaynerchuk's, we probably have to do a lot more work ourselves. This is to your advantage when starting off, because being closer to the creation and posting process means you have better insight into how the content is received.

Whenever you post 'micro' snippets of your pillar content, be sure to listen to your audience's comments. Better yet, ask them in the caption "if anything is unclear" or to "leave a time-stamp for your favorite part of the video!" Remember, if you want to grow, you have to post what your audience wants to see. It's a lot easier to know what they want to see when they tell you outright. And since it's coming from *your* pillar content, it's a message that you care to spread.

Once you have learned what your audience is most interested in, you can create more pieces of media around that insight to be distributed on social media. Think of it like the blindfolded free throw:

You just took 100 blindfolded shots in a row, and left a camera setup to record your form and results. You may have air-balled 60 of the 100, but what did you do differently on the 30 shots that hit rim? What about the eight that "just had a bad bounce?" And what about the two that spun twice in the rim, just before somehow missing? You could call the 10 close calls luck, or you could watch the video and find what you did differently. If you have greater financial means, you can hire a coach to watch the video and tell you what you did differently. If you have these means and are dedicated, you can hire a coach to be with you when you watch the video—and give you critiques in real time.

The art and science of scoring a blindfolded free throw is akin to posting on social media. Volume and critiques are all that you can operate on. You have to post with the hope that you will go viral, just as you need to shoot with the hope of scoring.

In the long run, you'll end up at your own equilibrium.

CHAPTER 13

MY NEXT STEPS — JOIN ME!

So all of that stuff I wrote about is cool, right? But I didn't give you a lot of immediately actionable tips. That's because the most immediately actionable tips aren't evergreen, and by the time you read this book, many that I'd give would likely already be outdated.

"Perfection is achieved, not when there is nothing more to add, but when there is nothing left to take away."

-ANTOINE DE SAINT-EXUPERY

To be absolutely transparent: I'm sitting in my living room right now, the day before I turn this manuscript in for copy-editing, and completely changing this final chapter. My goal in writing this book, and turning it into my pillar content, is almost entirely based on the people I will be able to have conversations with as a result.

What lights a fire under me is interesting conversations, with people who are much smarter than me and have already achieved whatever my goal that day, week, month, or year happens to be. I love being the dumbest and least successful person in the room, and to this point in my life have been pretty good at being in that position often. Which isn't to say that I'm not intelligent, it's just to say that I seek out people who are better than me at what I'm trying to do—and do my best to copy what I can.

One of those people I was fortunate enough to connect with recently is QuHarrison Terry. Among a seemingly endless list of accolades, QuHarrison was a Top LinkedIn Voice in Technology from 2016-2018. Oh yeah, in 2016 he also graduated from college... as an undergraduate with a degree in computer science. What really caught my attention when I received a connection request from him, though, was his LinkedIn headline.

"Growth Marketing at Mark Cuban Companies." I remember seeing it and thinking, okay—this guy knows his shit.

I didn't reach out with the goal of interviewing him, but 10-15 minutes into talking about emerging tech use-cases, the metaverse, platform agnosticism, and his new brand Inevitable Human, it was clear that I HAD to get some insight from him.

QuHarrison doesn't champion sharing your story on any platform in particular, but he did tell me, "If you have an opinion, that makes you a leader. Don't worry too much about your long-term voice, just try your best to create daily. Realistically, you'll find yourself posting almost daily. I actually have a three-pronged strategy that I use for LinkedIn."

And I thought to myself.... SCORE! This guy is platform agnostic, works in multiple niches I have an affinity towards, and is kicking ass in them. His three-pronged strategy is SO simple, and closer to perfection than what I had written before completely changing this chapter.

I found his strategy so special because it's completely devoid of tips and tricks that only work temporarily. His strategy is evergreen, can be applied across mediums, and will survive a shift to new platforms.

1. Connect with people you know.

- On LinkedIn in particular, you don't want to be a stranger in your own network. If you don't KNOW your audience, what's the point? It's not all about the SIZE of your audience, it's about the quality of your connection to them. "I realized in college that I was 2nd connections with Obama on LinkedIn. This guy named Steve was connected with him. That 2nd connection would have meant nothing if I hadn't actually known Steve." -QuHarrison Terry

2. Leave thoughtful comments on other people's posts.
   - If you want to create connections with a like-minded audience, you should comment and add to the conversation on posts that are getting a lot of attention in your niche. Your goal here is to create dialogue. "I hit you up because you left an engaging comment on Gary Vaynerchuk's post. If you dropped a wave emoji… nah." -QuHarrison Terry

3. When you share, have a purpose.
   - QuHarrison framed this as if you're trying to spark a conversation at a dinner party. If you're sharing an article you found interesting on the Internet, how would you bring it up to spark a conversation at a dinner party? "800,000 views to your content ain't sh*t. I'd much rather have 40 billionaires who are interested in having the conversation see it."

Of course, this is a simple strategy, and there are so many things you can do to boost each action along the way. But perfection is the enemy of execution—you don't need to start out perfect, and it actually makes for a more interesting story if you learn along the way.

So many creators, myself included, are worried about their "voice." Whether it's fear of judgement, lack of concrete knowledge, or imposter syndrome when speaking as a voice of authority in your field—you're not alone and I'm sorry you feel that way. I do too.

BUT this is where you will find so much value in using social media.

Document, and be yourself. I, for one, am endlessly curious… and have pretty ridiculous ADHD. I'm a couple of years into the fields of digital marketing and advertising, but I'm no pundit… yet.

My hope is for social media to allow me to connect with people who ARE pundits, like QuHarrison, and learn everything I can from them. I'm going to continue to share my content and my insights with the goal of learning from people who know more than me. The more you learn, the more you realize you don't know. So if you finished reading this book with more questions than when you began, I feel like I served my purpose in sparking your curiosities.

Coming into writing this book, I'd hoped I'd be able to share the secrets of going viral on the Internet with all of you. I was aiming to answer the billion-dollar question on my first go (and if you don't get that money-figure reference, that's what Dollar Shave Club sold for). Instead, I feel like I've only answered thousand, and ten-thousand-dollar questions.

This book is my baby, but it's not my masterpiece. That comes later. For now, on my original topic of virality:

"A bird doesn't sing because it has an answer, it sings because it has a song."

-MARY ANGELOU

Thank you for listening to my song. And I hope you got some answers along the way.

If you have any questions, comments… or really anything you want to talk about – please reach out. I'd love to hear from you.

At the time of writing, I'm most responsive to messages on LinkedIn and Instagram—and one from you would make my day.

WORKS CITED

Pre-Intro

Avella, J. and Lebowitz, S. (2019). *Valedictorians rarely become rich and famous — here's why the average millionaire's college GPA is 2.9.* Business Insider.

Bishop, G. (2017). *Unfuck yourself.* London: Yellow Kite.

Intro

Blakely, L. (2017). *How a $4,500 YouTube Video Turned Into a $1 Billion Company.* Inc.com.

Dirnhuber, J. (2019). *Children turn backs on traditional careers in favour of internet fame, study finds.* The Sun.

Forbes. (2019). *Rory O'Reilly, 21, Kieran O'Reilly, 20.*

NASA. (2019). *Astronaut Candidate Jonny Kim.*

Vaynerchuk, G. (2017). *Cheering for Optimism and The Internet.* GaryVaynerchuk.com.

www.dictionary.com. (2019). *Definition of viral | Dictionary.com.*

Chapter 1

Statista. (2019). *Social networks: average daily usage by U.S. users 2021 | Statista.*

Chapter 2

Gillies, D. (2012). *Marshall McLuhan's Legacy in Culture and Scholarship | The Canadian Encyclopedia.* Thecanadianencyclopedia.ca.

Gordon, T. (2002). *Who was Marshall McLuhan? – The Estate of Marshall McLuhan.* Marshallmcluhan.com.

McLuhan, M., Agel, J. and Fiore, Q. (2008). *The medium is the massage.* London: Penguin Books.

Shachtman, N. (2002). *Honoring Wired's Patron Saint.* WIRED.

Chapter 3

Stout, D. (2019). *Social Media Statistics: Top Social Networks by Popularity.*

Chapter 5

Choi, C. (2010). *How 'Jaws' Forever Changed Our View of Great White Sharks.* livescience.com.

Chapter 6

Brunson, R. (2015). *DotCom Secrets -The Underground Playbook for Growing Your Company Online.* Morgan James.

Gallo, C. (2016). *Dollar Shave Club VC: How An Improv Comic Schooled A 115-Year-Old Brand.* Forbes.com.

Ransom, D. (2015). *How Dollar Shave Club Rode a Viral Video to Sales Success.* Inc.com.

Chapter 7

Breihan, T. (2012). *Mixtape Of The Week: Joey Bada$$ 1999*. Stereogum.

Complex. (2012). *Who Is Joey Bada$$?Learning to Rap*.

Malek, R. (2018). *Joey Bada$$ tells Rami Malek how he uses his music to stand for something bigger - Interview Magazine*. Interview Magazine.

Chapter 8

Gladwell, M. (2008). *Outliers*. Little, Brown and Company.

Kahneman, D. (2011). *Thinking, fast and slow*. New York: Random House Audio.

The Economist. (2017). *The world's most valuable resource is no longer oil, but data*.

Chapter 10

Press, A. (2018). *7-year-old toy reviewer on YouTube becomes a toy himself*. Whdh.com.

Robehmed, N. and Burg, M. (2019). *Highest-Paid YouTube Stars 2018: Markiplier, Jake Paul, PewDiePie And More.* Forbes.com.

Schmidt, S. (2017). *6-year-old made $11 million in one year reviewing toys on YouTube.* Washington Post.

Statista. (2019). *U.S. YouTube ad advertising revenues 2020 | Statista.*

Chapter 12

Vaynerchuk, Gary. 2019. "The Garyvee Content Strategy: How To Grow And Distribute Your Brand'S Social Media Content". *Garyvaynerchuk.Com.*

Made in the USA
Middletown, DE
11 January 2020